The Landscape of Britain

The Cotswold Collection

William Fricker

Photography: William Fricker
Text: William Fricker

First published in the United Kingdom, in 2010, by
Goldeneye, Unit 10, Chivenor Business Park, Barnstaple,
North Devon EX31 4AY.
Tel: 01271 813040

www.goldeneyeguides.co.uk

Maps copyright © Goldeneye, 2010
Book design and layout: Camouka
Editor: Caroline Patterson
Photographic Scans & Repro: Flora Fricker
Cover: Sherborne Brook

ISBN Number 9 781859 651 995

Printed in China by 1010 Printing International Ltd

GOLDENEYE

To Caroline, my beloved Cotswold girl, whose inspiration, enthusiasm and faith for this project has never faltered.

▲ Coln Valley   Laburnum Walk, Barnsley House

Chasing The Light...

This book of photography is a testament to my long relationship with this enchanting corner of England. Until moving to North Devon, the Cotswolds was my base for 30 years.

For 20 of those years I walked, drove and cycled around the area; researching, writing and photographing for Goldeneye maps and guides. I played cricket in many of the towns and villages, and sampled many a brew in the local hostelries. I eventually married Caroline, my Cotswold girl, and our wedding took place in Gloucester Cathedral, a privilege rarely granted to those outside the Church. It so happened that her grandfather had been Vicar of Guiting Power for 25 years.

My parents and father-in-law still live in the Cotswolds providing me with an ongoing base. Over the years, I have come to know the area intimately and have developed a great fondness for it. It is thanks to my ever-supportive wife, that I am now, at last, encouraged to produce this book of photography.

I am often asked for advice on capturing the perfect picture and my instant response would be that the camera used is incidental. Of course, you must not take this too literally as a brand new digital SLR camera is better able to do the photographer's work than an old manual model. What I mean is that your knowledge of the subject matter; the weather, the seasons and times of day; as well as clever use of a tripod, are far more important. If you do not have a good understanding of the above items, perfect pictures are only ever going to come about by chance. You will achieve some quality images but you will never reach the holy grail of photographers: consistently brilliant photos. I must put my hand up here and say that, in reality, no photographer in the world takes only brilliant photos as there is always an element of luck involved – one cannot control the appearance of other mortals nor the sudden changes in weather that can make our countryside so startlingly different from day to day. The introduction of digital cameras is of benefit to both amateur and professional photographers as it allows you to experiment, take far too many photos and then edit them harshly in the cold glow of your computer screen.

Until the introduction of digital photography most of my images were taken with a Nikon FE, a brilliantly robust and simple manual SLR, ably assisted by my trusty Manfrotto tripod. I must have got through at least six bodies over a twenty-year period and was a little hesitant, at first, to be fully sold into the use of digital technology, but I have been truly bowled over by the flexibility and practicality of this medium. I started using a Fuji S1 Pro due to its compatibility with my lenses and because of its wonderful range of colour. Its slowness was a complete bore. However, I now use a Nikon D300 and its speed and quality of tone are awesome. To get the best out of it, you must get to know your camera's mechanics and idiosyncrasies as if they are second nature to you.

I am from the school of 'natural photography' and my intent or style has always been to try and represent the subject, be it a building or a field of sheep, in the best possible light, and from a perspective that you, the reader, will recognise as you pass it by. I rarely use filters to change the image into something unrecognizable and, although I admire those photographers who can create a stunning image out of a dull reality, this has never been my aim. I believe photography, or rather the consistent capture of great photographic images to be a truly difficult task. It has taken me

many years to reach my current level of professionalism and so I continue to doff my hat at the brilliance of some of my peers (amateur and professional) and offer words of encouragement to all the budding photographers out there.

When all is said and done, just get out there, camera in hand, have fun, persevere and whatever your ambitions, I do hope that you find enjoyment and perhaps a little inspiration from the images in this book.

William Fricker,
Buckland Barton, September 2010

February Snowdrops, Rococo Garden, Painswick

An introduction

What and where is the region known as the Cotswolds? To those who know it, this may seem like a silly question. However, it is a place that manifests itself in many different ways to different people. Even down to the area they would define as the Cotswolds on a map. To some fashionistas, and magazine editors, the Cotswolds runs comparison to the New York Hamptons and Tuscany. Whilst to others the name is synonymous with wool and hunting, stone walls and majestic churches. From my point of view and for the purposes of this book, the area stretches from Chipping Campden in the north to Bath in the south, and from Gloucester to Witney, west to east. The book also features Oxford (because the building's materials are cut from Cotswold limestone) although it is not technically considered part of the Cotswolds.

The Cotswolds derives its name from two Saxon words: 'Cote' - sheep fold, and 'Wold' - bare hill. This references the importance of sheep in the development of the area. And, it is to the Cotswold Lion sheep that one must look for the origin of wealth and endeavour that brought prosperity to this region.

The Cotswolds region is perched on the central section of a ridge of oolitic limestone. The geological structure has thus had a profound and lasting affect on the landscape, and 'look' of the area. The oolitic limestone that forms these hills has the appearance of 1,000s of tiny balls, like fish roe and is between 200 and 175 million years old.

This ridge has been tilted on its side and is run off with streams and river valleys that lead off in a south-easterly direction to feed the Thames basin. On the western edge the scarp is steep in places with outcrops of rounded hills, notably Cam Long Down and Bredon Hill and makes for fine walking country and pleasing views across to the Malvern Hills and Wales.

Neolithic Man found refuge on these hills from the swamps of the Severn and Thames flood plains. The *Celtic Dobunni* tribe established hill forts where they farmed, bartered their crafts and founded coinage before the Romans arrived. They were not a warlike tribe like their neighbours the *Silurians* (Welsh) and eased into a compatible relationship with the conquering Romans to build *Corinium Dobunnorum* (Cirencester) into the second largest Roman settlement in Britain with a populace of 12,000 inhabitants.

The Saxon farmer laid the foundations of prosperity for the medieval wool merchants, and it was these merchants who built the great 'Wool' churches and the great manor houses.

More latterly, the Cotswolds has come to represent elegance and wealth. In the C18, Bath and Cheltenham epitomised the elegance, hedonism and splendour of the Georgian era.

The landscape is rich in imagery: dry-stone walls divide the vast, sweeping sheep pastures and lazy, winding, trout streams meander through the rich pastureland. And, scattered across this landscape you will come across quaint hamlets undisturbed by coach, sightseer or time itself. All this makes for an idyllic scene rarely bettered in England.

Glouceste . County . General Maps

GLOCESTRIÆ
Siue Claudiocestriæ Comitat' Claudy
Cæsaris nomine ad huc celebrat'
verus Typus atq; effigies
An' Dñi 1577

VIGORNIÆ PARS

HEREFORDIÆ PARS

MONVMETHENSIS PARS

OCCIDENS

PARS

Sabrina flu.

WIL... NIÆ

SOMERSETENSIS PARS

MERIDIES

AVGVS SCVLP

Contents

Irises, Barnsley House Garden

Bath

Arguably the finest city in England; Bath owes its fame to the discovery of hot springs in 863BC. The Bath Springs were developed in about 60-70 AD by the Romans who built a wall around the 23 acre site naming it Aquae Sulis. It prospered for 400 years until the Romans withdrew from Britain in 410 AD. The city saw much prosperity in the Middle Ages from the sale of Cotswold wool. But the heyday of Bath began over a 40-year period when three men of immense vision transformed the city with a populace of 3,000 into the Georgian city of 30,000 citizens. They were Beau Nash (Master of Ceremonies, manners and fashion), John Wood, (architect), and Ralph Allen, (benefactor, financier and quarry owner who supplied the building materials). In a city of such architectural beauty, of particular note are The Circus and The Royal Crescent.

Originally named King's Circus, The Circus was the vision of John Wood the Elder and was built between 1754 and 1768. It was his intention to create a classical Palladian architectural landscape inspired by Rome's Colosseum. The Circus is made up of 33 terraced houses. Thomas Gainsborough lived in No.17 from 1765-1774. On the architect's death, The Circus was completed by his son, John Wood the Younger. The Royal Crescent was also built by him, between 1767 and 1774. Today the 30 original homes are split into flats, houses and a hotel, and many are privately owned.

Pulteney Road

The Circus, Bath

Bath Abbey, Abbey Churchyard ▲   Stairway to Heaven ▶

The current site of the Church of St Peter and St Paul, otherwise known as Bath Abbey, has been the home of three churches: an Anglo-Saxon church in 757 and a Norman Cathedral in 1090 but later in 1137 much of this was destroyed by fire. Today's building was founded in 1499 to replace the ruin damaged in the fire. But it had again to be rebuilt in 1611 following Henry VIII's Dissolution of the Monasteries. In simple architectural terms it can be described as Perpendicular Gothic and cruciform in plan. The fan vaulting of the Nave is very fine and was designed by Robert and William Vertue, designers of Henry VII's chapel in Westminster Abbey. It was never finished until Gilbert Scott completed the original designs in the 1860s. Note the Stairway to Heaven on the West Front.

◄ Pulteney Bridge

River Avon, Bathampton ▲

River Avon, Bathampton

Dyrham Park

View from Haresfield Beacon

The Chantry ▲

Bradford-on-Avon

Situated in the Vale of Pewsey and on an adjoining hillside, Bradford-on-Avon is the last Cotswold town in west Wiltshire close to the borders of Somerset. The town centre is full of narrow streets lined with shops as well as impressive Roman and Norman architecture. It is dissected by the River Avon and the Kennet and Avon canal which provide a glimpse into the mill-related past of the town. The surrounding hillside is scattered with weavers' cottages of all shapes and sizes built in Cotswold stone.

Georgian Houses, Bradford-on-Avon ▲   Canal Wharf and Lock, Bradford-on-Avon ▶

Three-Arch Bridge, Castle Combe ▲

Castle Combe

One of the prettiest and most visited villages in the Cotswolds lies sheltered in a hidden valley surrounded by steep, wooded hills. In former times, it was an important medieval wool centre as evidenced by the weavers and clothiers' cottages that descend from the Market Cross to By Brook and the three-arch bridge.

▲ Lacock Cottage   Lacock Abbey ▶

Lacock ▲ ▶

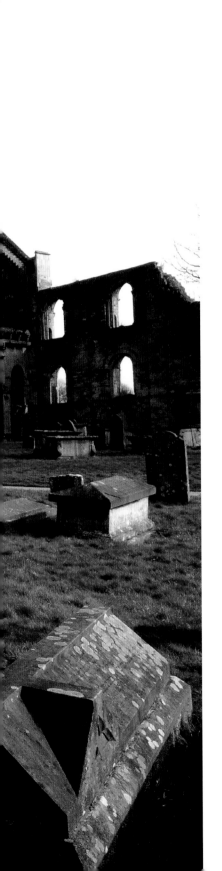

Westonbirt Arboretum ▲ ▶

Tetbury

A prosperous town with a fine Market House and the austere Church of St Mary. The town's recent claim to fame has been due to its proximity to Highgrove, Prince Charles' home at Doughton. Today, it is the Cotswold's major centre for antiques and a popular destination due to the recent growth of new shops, galleries and places to eat and drink. The Woolsack Races on May Bank Holiday are fun to watch and cause great merriment if you are not forced to carry the heavy woolsack.

Tetbury Church ▲ Chavenage

▲ Market House

◄ Hoar Frost, Severn Vale   The Wildfowl and Wetlands Trust, Slimbridge ▲

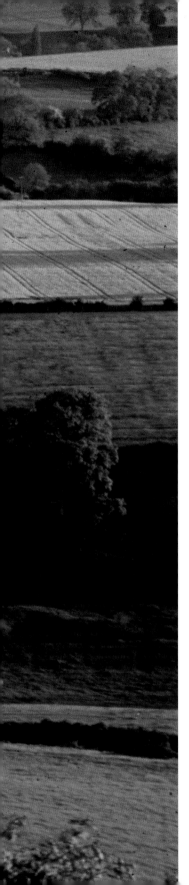

◄ Below Coaley Peak

Cam Long Down ▲

▲ Painswick Churchyard ▶

▲ Rococo Garden, Painswick

▲ Rococo Garden, Painswick

Prinknash Abbey Estate ▲

Bagendon Cottage ▲

◄ Saltridge Wood, Sheepscombe   Bagendon Church ▲

Sapperton Church

The Parish Church of St Kenelm. There has been a church here since the C12. What one notices today are the extraordinary wood-carvings on the bench ends. These were taken from the manor house demolished in the C18. The alabaster couple facing each other are Sir Henry Poole and his wife.

Edgeworth ▲ ▶

Miserden Churchyard ▲

Duntisbourne Rouse Church ▲

A group of isolated hamlets dotted along a beautiful valley. Duntisbourne Abbots stands at the head of the valley. The road to Duntisbourne Leer runs adjacent to the stream, the Dunt Brook flowing through each hamlet. Middle Duntisbourne and Duntisbourne Rouse are two farming hamlets, the latter famous for its idyllic Saxon church.

▲ Middle Duntisbourne Barns   Duntisbourne Abbots Churchyard ▶

The Duntisbournes

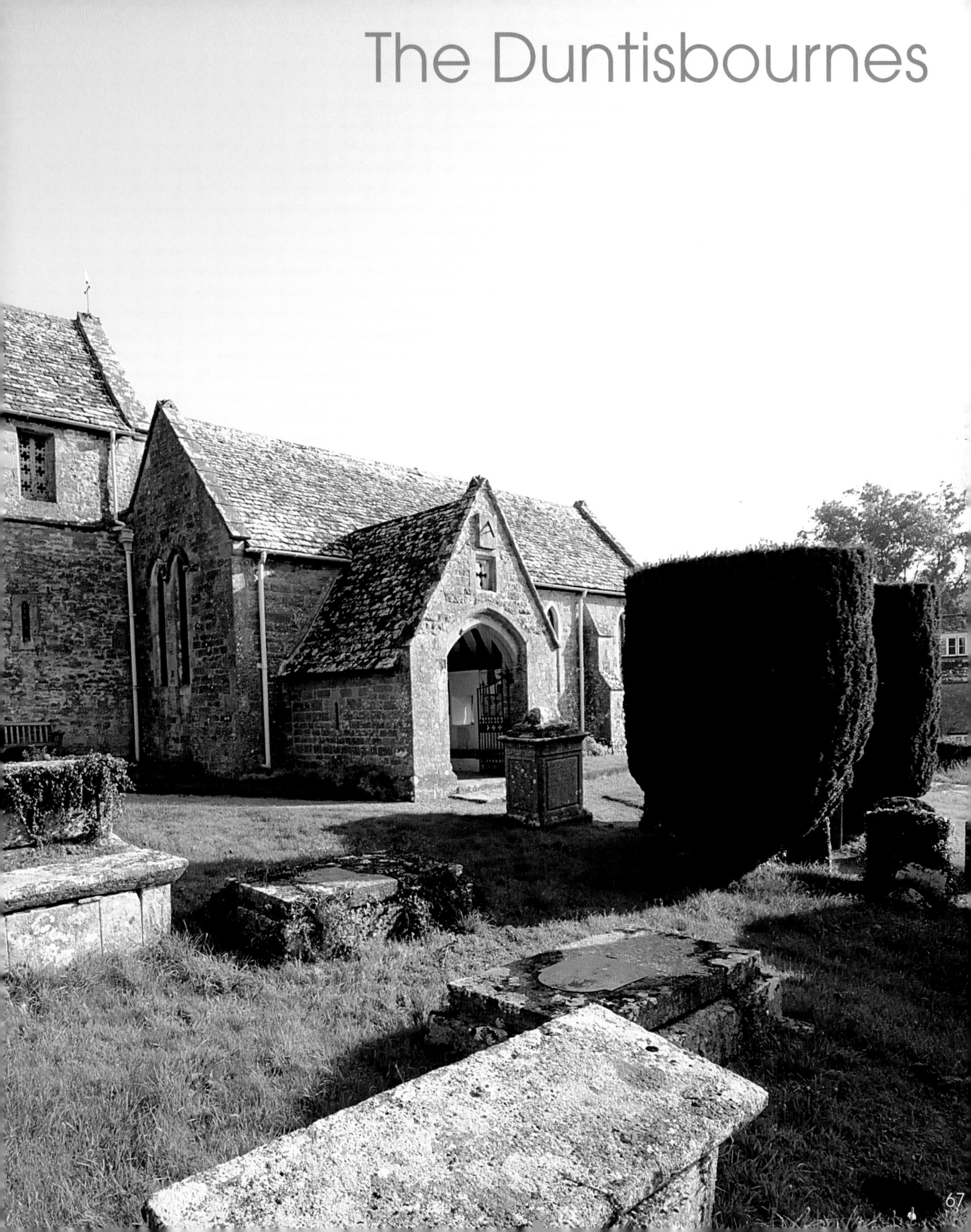

Dovecote — Middle Duntisbourne

▲ Frocester Estate Barn   Doorway, Middle Duntisbourne ▶

Owlpen Manor, Uley

Cirencester

One of the finest and most affluent towns in the Cotswolds lies surrounded by a plethora of attractive villages whose populace (often second home owners) tend to shop and hobnob in Ciren (as the locals call it). The smart shops and bars reflect the riches of its patrons. As the Roman town Corinium, it became the second largest Roman town (after London) in Britain. Its strategic position at the confluence of the major routes (the Fosse Way, Ermin Way and Akeman Street) combined with the vast rolling sheep pastures brought great wealth in the Middle Ages.

◄ Parish Church of St John the Baptist

Roman Carving, Corinium Museum ▲

Cirencester

Beaufort Polo Club, Westonbirt

◄ River Coln, Coln St Dennis   Laburnum Walk, Barnsley House ▲

Colin Rogers

Coates

◄ ▲ Swan and Signets, Bibury

Bibury

William Morris described Bibury as "One of the prettiest villages in England", and few would argue with him. As a honey-pot village made up of rose-covered cottages set behind idyllic kitchen gardens it attracts the crowds. Running parallel to the pavement is the River Coln inhabited by swans, duckling and trout.

The Parish Church of St Mary the Virgin, Fairford

This perfect, late C15 Perpendicular church is world-famous for the outstanding 28 stained glass windows depicting scenes from Genesis to the Last Judgement. Of further interest are the carved misericords and recumbent brasses, and the C6 Saxon cemetery. Set in an attractive market town on the tranquil River Coln.

Geese on Song, Coln Valley, Bibury

Lupins. The Glebe, Bourton-on-the-Water

Bourton-on-the-Water

One of the most popular beauty spots in the area, sometimes described as 'The Venice of the Cotswolds', because the River Windrush that runs parallel to the main street is spanned with low, graceful bridges. The village is full of attractive houses and is built above Salmonsbury Camp, a Roman settlement. A short walk from the village centre takes you to Bourton Lakes, a solitary refuge to wild fowl.

Sherborne Brook in Frost ▲

◂ ▴ Cotswold Farm Park

Chedworth Woods

▲ Chedworth Woods at Dawn   Mosaic, Chedworth Roman Villa ▶

▲ Guiting Church   Diana's View of Guiting's Landscape ▶

Wyck Rissington

The Brandy Cask
FREE HOUSE

MORRIS CLOWN
FREE HOUSE

The JOCKEY
Free House

FREE HOUSE
FOSTONS ASH

MILLERS ARMS
WADWORTH

The Maytime Inn
FREE HOUSE
& RESTAURANT

The George Hotel
HOOK NORTON
ALES
EST 1849

THE TUNNEL HOUSE

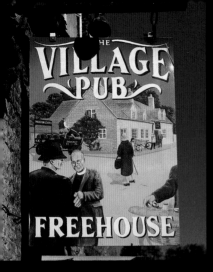

THE VILLAGE PUB

FREEHOUSE

The SWAN

The SMOKING DOG

THE MER...

FREE HOUSE

The Hunt on CAT & CUSTARD POT Day

The Slaughters

Lower Slaughter is one of the most popular villages in the Cotswolds. Little bridges cross the Eye Stream which runs beside rows of golden cottages. The much painted C19 redbrick Corn Mill stands on the western edge of the village. Upper Slaughter is a couple of miles upstream and has an old Manor House once lived in by the Slaughter family, an old Post Office with a beautiful kitchen garden and, along a lane past the church, a ford crosses the stream hidden beneath lush greenery.

Lower Slaughter Manor ▲ Lower Slaughter

Abbotswood, Lower Swell

Alliums, Barnsley House ▲   Sezincote House and Garden, Moreton-in-Marsh ▶

Bourton House Garden, Bourton-on-the-Hill

Stow-on-the-Wold

With a name like this it is bound to attract visitors, and it has, and does so to this day, for with its exposed position at the intersection of eight roads (one being the Fosse Way) Stow has been party to some momentous events in history. The Romans used Stow as an encampment and route centre. The Viking merchants traded down the Fosse Way, but it was the Saxon hill farmers who laid the foundations for the fleece which created wealth for the wool merchants who used the great Market Place for sheep sales of 20,000, or more.

Sudeley Castle

One of the great houses of Gloucestershire, this was the original home of the Seymour family. Katherine Parr, widow of Henry VIII lived here and lies buried in the chapel. Later bought by the Dent-Brocklehursts who made their wealth from glove-making. The interior has a fine collection of needlework, furniture and many great master paintings. All surrounded by award-winning gardens, designed in part, by the late Rosemary Verey of Barnsley House.

◀ Hailes Abbey, Winchcombe   Deadmanbury Gate, Winchcombe ▲

131

Gargoyles

The word gargoyle is a derivation from the French word gargouille meaning throat or pipe. Carved gargoyles were invented to channel water off, or away, from the roofs of buildings. The reason for the strange and often ugly designs is open to conjecture. Some believe they are caricatures of the clergy, or that they are there to ward off evil spirits. Others believe they are transformed into ghosts and ghoulies at night!

Gargoyles, Winchcombe Church

Snowshill

This charming and unspoilt hilltop village is a short distance from Broadway.

There's a striking church, a pub and a row of much photographed cottages opposite Snowshill Manor. Once home to the eccentric Charles Pagent Wade, it now houses some 22,000 items from his collection of toys, musical instruments, bicycles, clocks and samurai armour.

Snowshill Manor ▲

▲ Snowshill Manor

Stanton

Situated at the foot of Shenbarrow Hill, Stanton is an un-commercial and consequently peaceful village. Little changed in 300 years and well restored by Sir Philip Scott, 1903-37, Stanton has several C16 and C17 buildings as well as a medieval cross.

Withington

Stanway

This village is dominated by the outstanding Manor House.

In its grounds stands one of the country's finest tithe barns designed with the Golden Proportion in mind and across the road a thatched cricket pavilion, set on staddle stones. The beautiful Gatehouse is C17, and was probably built by Timothy Strong of Little Barrington. It bears the arms of the Tracy family. The little Church of St Peter has C14 origins and some amusing gargoyles.

145

Cheltenham

A smaller version of Bath, often described as 'the most complete Regency town in England'. Elegant Regency buildings overlook the crescents, squares, tree-lined avenues and spacious parks. Cheltenham remains, in historic terms, a young town of a mere 300 years. It grew as a spa after George III had approved the waters in 1788. Thereafter, distinguished visitors such as George Handel and Samuel Johnson came to be revitalised. The Promenade is one of the most attractive shopping streets in England which becomes progressively more independent and up-market as you head west towards Montpelier. Cheltenham is proud of its calendar of festivals: Antique, Folk, Greenbelt, Jazz, Literature, Music, Science, Wychwood...but it is during the Cheltenham Festival of National Hunt Racing which takes place in March that the town takes on a carnival atmosphere.

Lansdown Terrace ▶

Cheltenham

▲ Pittville Pump Room   Devil's Chimney, Leckhampton ▶

Cleeve Hill ▲ ▶

159

Barrow Wake, Birdlip Hill ▲

Gloucester

The county town of Gloucestershire was originally a port connected to the tidal Bristol Channel and a strategic point developed by the Romans into the fort Glevum. Today, it is not unusual to spy tall ships at the Old Docks where the spectacular C19 warehouses have been restored. This ancient city is dominated by the magnificent Cathedral Church of St Peter, and the Holy and Undivided Trinity. Without exception the most magnificent building in Gloucestershire, and one of the finest of all English cathedrals. Its architecture is Romanesque, with some early Perpendicular. The East Window behind the altar had at its installation the largest display of medieval stained glass in the world and dates from 1350. The same year, fan vaulting was invented here at Gloucester and its intricate design covers the roof of the cloisters.

The Cloisters Fan Vaulting and The Central Spire, Gloucester Cathedral

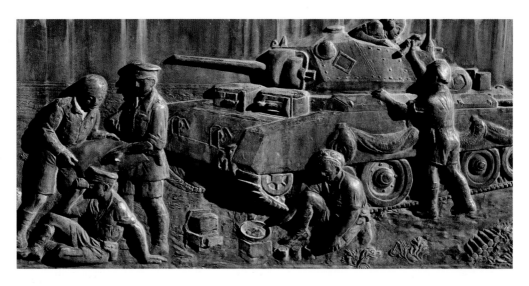

▲ The Royal Gloucester's Memorial, College Green   Gloucester Docks ▶

▲ College Green   Bishop Hooper's Monument ▶

Tewkesbury Abbey

Founded in 1087 by the nobleman Robert Fitzhamon. However, the present building was started in 1102 to house Benedictine monks. The Norman Abbey was consecrated in 1121. The Nave and roof finished in the C14 in the Decorated style. Much is Early English and Perpendicular, although it is larger than many cathedrals and has according to Pevsner, 'the finest Romanesque Tower in England'. The Abbey opens its doors to three major music festivals: Musica Deo Sacra, the Three Choirs Festival and the Cheltenham Music Festival.

The Nave, Tewkesbury Abbey

Tewkesbury

Broadway

'The Painted Lady of the Cotswolds'

is a term often used to describe this beautiful village.
The honey-coloured stone captivates the visitor today as it did in the C19 when William
Morris and his pre-Raphaelite friends settled here. A slow walk up the High Street will
reveal some large and impressive houses that have been homes to Edward Elgar, JM Barrie
(Peter Pan), Ralph Vaughan Williams, Sir Gerald Navarro MP and Laura Ashley. Overlooked
by Broadway Tower, an C18 folly tower and country retreat of William Morris. On a clear day
12 counties can be seen from the top of the Tower.

◄ ▲ Broadway Tower

Broadway Cottages ▲

Topiary, St Eadburghs ▲

St Eadburghs ▲

▲ Broadway High Street

Hidcote Manor Gardens

Chipping Campden

A perfect example of a Cotswold town, containing many ancient and remarkable buildings. The harmony of Cotswold stone mirrors the town's prosperity in the Middle Ages. The Gabled Market Hall was built in 1627 by the wealthy landowner Sir Baptist Hicks whose mansion was burnt down in the Civil War, and the remains are the two lodges beside the Church. The Church of St James is a tall and statuesque 'Wool' church. William Grevel, one of the wealthiest wool merchants, is remembered in the church on a brass transcription which reads: 'the flower of the wool merchants of all England'. Opposite his house (Grevel's House) on the High Street is the Woolstaplers Hall, the meeting place for the fleece (staple) merchants.

Market Hall ▲

Parish Church of St James ▲   William Grevel's House ▶

Woolstapler's Hall ▲

◄ High Street

Seymour House ▲

Thatch Cottages, Westington ▲ ▶

◀▲ Broad Campden

Delphiniums, The Glebe, Bourton-on-the-Water

Broughton Castle

Home to the Lords Saye and Sele (Fiennes family), for over 600

years. Originally, a moated medieval manor house that was substantially enlarged in the C16. The interior has a wealth of interest; magnificent plaster ceilings, fine panelling and fireplaces but it is to the exterior that one is drawn to – the reflections in the moat and the multi-coloured borders.

Bliss Tweed Mill ▲　　Almshouses, Chipping Norton ▶

Great Tew

A sensationally beautiful village lined with ironstone cottages covered in thatch and stone tiles. Much of the village was designed by the Scottish architect John Claudius London. The Falkland Arms is named after Lord Falkland who lived here, and who died fighting for Charles I at the Battle of Newbury.

Burford

The first major Cotswold town you come to if travelling from the East.

Burford has a picturesque, wide High Street, with classical gables atop some gracious houses, which slopes down to the dreamy River Windrush. It's worth exploring the side streets, host to some splendid inns and pretty cottages and not to be missed, the fine Parish Church, notable for the intricately carved table tombs.

◄ ▲ Parish Church of St John the Baptist, Burford

▲ Windrush Valley in Frost

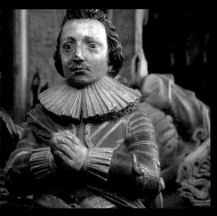

◄ ▲ Parish Church of St John the Baptist, Burford

Burford Reflections

Swinford Church ▲   Fettiplace Monument, Swinford ▶

EDMUND FETTIPLACE BARONET

In Memory of Sr Iohn Fettiplace Baronet.

IN MEMORY Iohn Fettiplace Esqr Guil Byrd Oxon fe

209

Minster Lovell

Arguably the most beautiful village in the Windrush Valley
where a fine C15 bridge leads to a street of pretty cottages and to the C15 Church which rests beside the
ancient Hall reputedly the haunted seat of the Lovell family. The Manor House has been associated with
the rhyme 'Mistletoe Bough'.

Minster Lovell Hall ▲

Oxford

Oxford was first occupied in Saxon times. It was initially known as *Oxenaforda*, (Ford of the Ox) as fords were more commonly used than bridges to cross the rivers, Cherwell and Thames. Now better known as 'The City of Dreaming Spires' due to the striking city skyline. A walk around the city will demonstrate the rich architectural heritage of Oxford, from the many buildings of the world-renowned University (first mentioned in C12 records) to Christopher Wren's Sheldonian Theatre, the iconic mid C18 Radcliffe Camera and the Venetian-inspired Bridge of Sighs.

Sheldonian Theatre ▲   The History of Science Museum ▶

Radcliffe Camera ▲   Bridge of Sighs ▶   Sheldonian Theatre ▶▶

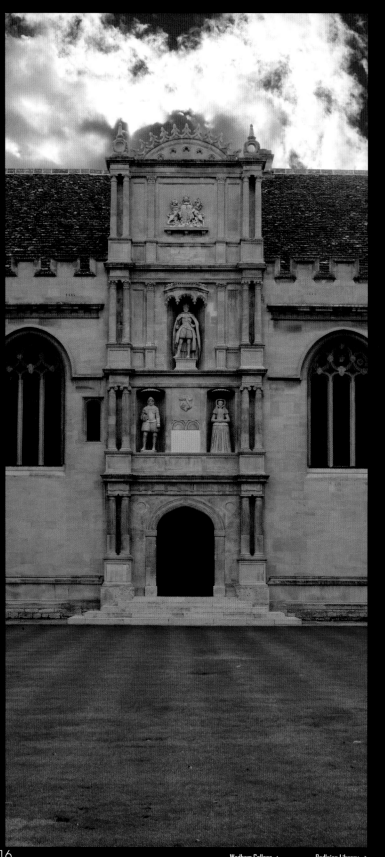

Wadham College ▲   Bodleian Library ▶

Hoar Frost, Westonbirt Arboretum

▲ Swalcliffe

▲ Yanworth

▲ Ashleworth

▲ Hartbury

Middle Littleton

▲ Bredon

Bredon

▲ Baughton

Location of Photographs
(By Page Numbers)

Stratford-on-Avon

Bidford
on Avon

Pershore

Great
Malvern

Evesham

Chipping
Campden | 182-183

Hereford

184-193

Shipston
on-Stour

Ledbury

176-181 Broadway

123 Moreton-
in-Marsh

224

142-147 | 134-137 | 124-125

Tewkesbury | 170-175

138-139

Chi
No

Winchcombe

128-129

126-127

200-20

Bishop's
Cleeve

130-133 | 1 | 108-109

158-159

Ross-on-Wye

4

120-121 | 102-103

Stow-on-the-W

110-111

Cheltenham

150-157

5 | 114-119

96-99, 194-195

162-169

160-161 | 2

Andoversford

Bourton-on-
the-Water

Gloucester

140-141

56-57 | 58

100-101

208

Northleach

204-207 Bur

8-9, 54-55

104-107

Painswick

64-65

Bibury

86-91, 94-95

30-31

10

66-69, 71

6, 80, 82-83

Cartertc

Stroud

62-63

59

7, 14-15, 81, 122

51

70

60-61

Fairford

Cirencester

Lechlade

52-53

Nailsworth

84-85 | 74-77

92-93

Dursley

Faringdon

72-73

46-47 Tetbury

Highworth

Wotton-under-Edge

Westonbirt | 44-45, 48-49, 78-79, 218-219

Malmesbury | 42-43

Swindon

Yate

Castle Combe

Wootton
Bassett

Wroughton

36-37

28-29 Marshfield

Chippenham

Portishead

Bristol

Corsham

Lacock

Calne

Marlboroug

Clevedon

38-41

Keynsham

16-27 Bath

Bradford-
on-Avon

Melksham

Devizes

Pewsey

32-35

Trowbridge

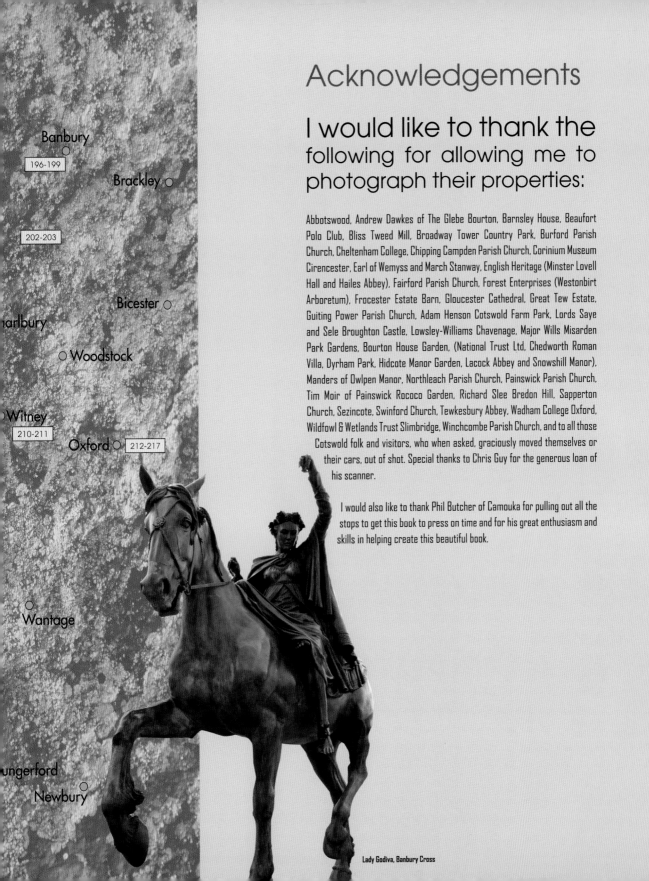

Acknowledgements

I would like to thank the following for allowing me to photograph their properties:

Abbotswood, Andrew Dawkes of The Glebe Bourton, Barnsley House, Beaufort Polo Club, Bliss Tweed Mill, Broadway Tower Country Park, Burford Parish Church, Cheltenham College, Chipping Campden Parish Church, Corinium Museum Cirencester, Earl of Wemyss and March Stanway, English Heritage (Minster Lovell Hall and Hailes Abbey), Fairford Parish Church, Forest Enterprises (Westonbirt Arboretum), Frocester Estate Barn, Gloucester Cathedral, Great Tew Estate, Guiting Power Parish Church, Adam Henson Cotswold Farm Park, Lords Saye and Sele Broughton Castle, Lowsley-Williams Chavenage, Major Wills Misarden Park Gardens, Bourton House Garden, (National Trust Ltd, Chedworth Roman Villa, Dyrham Park, Hidcote Manor Garden, Lacock Abbey and Snowshill Manor), Manders of Owlpen Manor, Northleach Parish Church, Painswick Parish Church, Tim Moir of Painswick Rococo Garden, Richard Slee Bredon Hill, Sapperton Church, Sezincote, Swinford Church, Tewkesbury Abbey, Wadham College Oxford, Wildfowl & Wetlands Trust Slimbridge, Winchcombe Parish Church, and to all those Cotswold folk and visitors, who when asked, graciously moved themselves or their cars, out of shot. Special thanks to Chris Guy for the generous loan of his scanner.

I would also like to thank Phil Butcher of Camouka for pulling out all the stops to get this book to press on time and for his great enthusiasm and skills in helping create this beautiful book.

Banbury
196-199

Brackley

202-203

Bicester

harlbury

Woodstock

Witney
210-211

Oxford   212-217

Wantage

ungerford
Newbury

Lady Godiva, Banbury Cross

Biography

William Fricker was born in Somerset and educated at Stonyhurst College, Lancashire and in various places of learning in Austria and Germany. He has worked in the book publishing industry for over thirty years.

William first worked for William Collins (now Harper Collins) where he rose to become a creative director in their paperback division. A chance encounter with the travel writer and soldier, Patrick Leigh Fermor (*A Time of Gifts*) encouraged William to give up his career and follow a long-held ambition, to undertake a long distance walk. He set out to trek 4,000 miles across Europe (through France, The Alps and Italy, to Greece) along old mule tracks, footpaths and pilgrim's routes. William then made the return journey on a bicycle via North Africa, Spain and France. The journey took eleven months. The experience gave birth to an interest in photography, maps and travel guides, and for the past twenty years William has worked for Goldeneye compiling the photography and editorial for more than one hundred UK travel guides. He lives with his wife, Caroline, and their four children in North Devon.

Many of the images in this book are available as Fine Art Prints and Canvas Prints. For details please go to William Fricker's Photo Library at: www.williamfricker.com

◀ Bredon Hill, Kemerton